Name

Wishes and Comments

Name

Wishes and Comments

Name

Wishes and Comments

Name

Wishes and Comments

Name Wishes and Comments

Name Wishes and Comments

Name Wishes and Comments

Name Wishes and Comments

Name | Wishes and Comments

Name | Wishes and Comments

Name | Wishes and Comments

Name | Wishes and Comments

Name

Wishes and Comments

Name

Wishes and Comments

Name

Wishes and Comments

Name

Wishes and Comments

Name

Wishes and Comments

Name

Wishes and Comments

Name

Wishes and Comments

Name

Wishes and Comments

Name Wishes and Comments

Name Wishes and Comments

Name Wishes and Comments

Name Wishes and Comments

Name | Wishes and Comments

Name | Wishes and Comments

Name | Wishes and Comments

Name | Wishes and Comments

Name

Wishes and Comments

Name

Wishes and Comments

Name

Wishes and Comments

Name

Wishes and Comments

Name Wishes and Comments

Name Wishes and Comments

Name Wishes and Comments

Name Wishes and Comments

Name

Wishes and Comments

Name

Wishes and Comments

Name

Wishes and Comments

Name

Wishes and Comments

Name | Wishes and Comments

Name | Wishes and Comments

Name | Wishes and Comments

Name | Wishes and Comments

Name

Wishes and Comments

Name

Wishes and Comments

Name

Wishes and Comments

Name

Wishes and Comments

Name Wishes and Comments

Name Wishes and Comments

Name Wishes and Comments

Name Wishes and Comments

Name

Wishes and Comments

Name

Wishes and Comments

Name

Wishes and Comments

Name

Wishes and Comments

Name | Wishes and Comments

Name | Wishes and Comments

Name | Wishes and Comments

Name | Wishes and Comments

Name

Wishes and Comments

Name

Wishes and Comments

Name

Wishes and Comments

Name

Wishes and Comments

Name Wishes and Comments

Name Wishes and Comments

Name Wishes and Comments

Name Wishes and Comments

Name Wishes and Comments

Name Wishes and Comments

Name Wishes and Comments

Name Wishes and Comments

Name Wishes and Comments

Name Wishes and Comments

Name Wishes and Comments

Name Wishes and Comments

Name Wishes and Comments

Name Wishes and Comments

Name Wishes and Comments

Name Wishes and Comments

Name

Wishes and Comments

Name

Wishes and Comments

Name

Wishes and Comments

Name

Wishes and Comments

Name Wishes and Comments

Name Wishes and Comments

Name Wishes and Comments

Name Wishes and Comments

Name | Wishes and Comments

Name | Wishes and Comments

Name | Wishes and Comments

Name | Wishes and Comments

Name Wishes and Comments

Name Wishes and Comments

Name Wishes and Comments

Name Wishes and Comments

Name

Wishes and Comments

Name

Wishes and Comments

Name

Wishes and Comments

Name

Wishes and Comments

Name Wishes and Comments

Name Wishes and Comments

Name Wishes and Comments

Name Wishes and Comments

Name

Wishes and Comments

Name

Wishes and Comments

Name

Wishes and Comments

Name

Wishes and Comments

Name | Wishes and Comments

Name | Wishes and Comments

Name | Wishes and Comments

Name | Wishes and Comments

Name Wishes and Comments

Name Wishes and Comments

Name Wishes and Comments

Name Wishes and Comments

Name

Wishes and Comments

Name

Wishes and Comments

Name

Wishes and Comments

Name

Wishes and Comments

Name

Wishes and Comments

Name

Wishes and Comments

Name

Wishes and Comments

Name

Wishes and Comments

Name

Wishes and Comments

Name

Wishes and Comments

Name

Wishes and Comments

Name

Wishes and Comments

Name

Wishes and Comments

Name

Wishes and Comments

Name

Wishes and Comments

Name

Wishes and Comments

Name

Wishes and Comments

Name

Wishes and Comments

Name

Wishes and Comments

Name

Wishes and Comments

Name

Wishes and Comments

Name

Wishes and Comments

Name

Wishes and Comments

Name

Wishes and Comments

Name

Wishes and Comments

Name

Wishes and Comments

Name

Wishes and Comments

Name

Wishes and Comments

Name | Wishes and Comments

Name | Wishes and Comments

Name | Wishes and Comments

Name | Wishes and Comments

Name

Wishes and Comments

Name

Wishes and Comments

Name

Wishes and Comments

Name

Wishes and Comments

Name Wishes and Comments

Name Wishes and Comments

Name Wishes and Comments

Name Wishes and Comments

Name

Wishes and Comments

Name

Wishes and Comments

Name

Wishes and Comments

Name

Wishes and Comments

Name Wishes and Comments

Name Wishes and Comments

Name Wishes and Comments

Name Wishes and Comments

Name Wishes and Comments

Name Wishes and Comments

Name Wishes and Comments

Name Wishes and Comments

Name Wishes and Comments

Name Wishes and Comments

Name Wishes and Comments

Name Wishes and Comments

Name

Wishes and Comments

Name

Wishes and Comments

Name

Wishes and Comments

Name

Wishes and Comments

Name

Wishes and Comments

Name

Wishes and Comments

Name

Wishes and Comments

Name

Wishes and Comments

Name

Wishes and Comments

Name

Wishes and Comments

Name

Wishes and Comments

Name

Wishes and Comments

Name Wishes and Comments

Name Wishes and Comments

Name Wishes and Comments

Name Wishes and Comments

Name Wishes and Comments

Name Wishes and Comments

Name Wishes and Comments

Name Wishes and Comments

Name Wishes and Comments

Name Wishes and Comments

Name Wishes and Comments

Name Wishes and Comments

Name Wishes and Comments

Name Wishes and Comments

Name Wishes and Comments

Name Wishes and Comments

Name Wishes and Comments

Name Wishes and Comments

Name Wishes and Comments

Name Wishes and Comments

Name

Wishes and Comments

Name

Wishes and Comments

Name

Wishes and Comments

Name

Wishes and Comments

Name

Wishes and Comments

Name

Wishes and Comments

Name

Wishes and Comments

Name

Wishes and Comments

Name

Wishes and Comments

Name

Wishes and Comments

Name

Wishes and Comments

Name

Wishes and Comments

Name

Wishes and Comments

Name

Wishes and Comments

Name

Wishes and Comments

Name

Wishes and Comments

Name

Wishes and Comments

Name

Wishes and Comments

Name

Wishes and Comments

Name

Wishes and Comments

Name

Wishes and Comments

Name

Wishes and Comments

Name

Wishes and Comments

Name

Wishes and Comments

Name | Wishes and Comments

Name | Wishes and Comments

Name | Wishes and Comments

Name | Wishes and Comments

Name | Wishes and Comments

Name | Wishes and Comments

Name | Wishes and Comments

Name | Wishes and Comments

Name | Wishes and Comments

Name | Wishes and Comments

Name | Wishes and Comments

Name | Wishes and Comments

Name

Wishes and Comments

Name

Wishes and Comments

Name

Wishes and Comments

Name

Wishes and Comments

Name

Wishes and Comments

Name

Wishes and Comments

Name

Wishes and Comments

Name

Wishes and Comments

Name

Wishes and Comments

Name

Wishes and Comments

Name

Wishes and Comments

Name

Wishes and Comments

Name

Wishes and Comments

Name

Wishes and Comments

Name

Wishes and Comments

Name

Wishes and Comments

Name | Wishes and Comments

Name | Wishes and Comments

Name | Wishes and Comments

Name | Wishes and Comments

Name

Wishes and Comments

Name

Wishes and Comments

Name

Wishes and Comments

Name

Wishes and Comments

Name Wishes and Comments

Name Wishes and Comments

Name Wishes and Comments

Name Wishes and Comments

Name Wishes and Comments

Name Wishes and Comments

Name Wishes and Comments

Name Wishes and Comments

Name

Wishes and Comments

Name

Wishes and Comments

Name

Wishes and Comments

Name

Wishes and Comments

www.ingramcontent.com/pod-product-compliance
Lightning Source LLC
Chambersburg PA
CBHW041607260326
41914CB00012B/1412
9781839903342